Soul Singing

Soul Singing

Poems by

Joseph Leary

© 2026 Joseph Leary. All rights reserved.
This material may not be reproduced in any form, published,
reprinted, recorded, performed, broadcast,
rewritten or redistributed without
the explicit permission of Joseph Leary.
All such actions are strictly prohibited by law.

Cover design by Shay Culligan
Cover image by Jack Leary
Author photo by Jack Leary

ISBN: 978-1-63980-797-0

Kelsay Books
502 South 1040 East, A-119
American Fork, Utah 84003
Kelsaybooks.com

to my brother Jack

Acknowledgments

I'm indebted to Kristin Leary Silber and my wife Susan for editing these works; and to poet Matthew Lippman, for his valuable guidance and encouragement; and my friend, author and literary agent Donna Eastman, for providing encouragement and expertise in the early going of my publications. And Andy Ryan, Andy Ryan Photography, Inc., for sharing his expertise in preparing Jack Leary's artwork for printing.

Thank you to the editors of the Massachusetts Bards Poetry Anthology 2025 for selecting my poem "Thinking of My Brother Jack" for inclusion.

Finally, my gratitude to the many readers who gave generously of their time and feedback: Patricia Shaw, Geraldine Lyons, Audrey Philbrick, Jennifer Leary Lynch, Dan Leary, Dave Leary, Carl Ristaino, Kristina Bray, and Nancy Rappa.

Contents

Walking the Bones	11
Thinking of My Brother Jack	15
The Warmth of Her Waist	17
The Rain of Sunshine	20
The Night the Music Changed	22
The Outing	26
Soul Singing	30
Saturday Morning Music	31
Riding the Chaparral with Thunder	32
Regarding Marriage	38
January Nights in Northern Virginia	40
Here They Come	44
You Can't Take It with You . . . Really	47
Flaming Mother in the Darkness	51
For Susan My Valentine	53
Images Flicker and Fade	54
Piecing the Universe Together	56
Hiroshima Bodhisattva	58
Time Traveler	64
Unseen Fingers	70
The Coils of Cochlea	72
On Memorial Day a Bluebird's Song Drifts in the Silence	74
She Whispers to Me	76
Dream Driving	78
Sadness in the Trees	81
A Perfect Woman to Be Dating	83
His Arms Open Wide	88

Walking the Bones

tend to the order
of things

mow the grass
wash the windows
mop the floor
clean the car
change the oil
replace the filters

brush your teeth
comb your hair
eat drink
walk the bones
flex the major muscles
inhale the elixir of life

cultivate humility
stop smile
listen chat
share your sacred attention
with another
in their crushing solitude

in your garden
give of yourself
to the citizens
of the earth
to basil parsley
oregano and dill

to tomatoes
red swollen
with juicy life
and wearing their
tiny tam o'shanter
caps of green
sitting safely
in gallon pails
tiny green shoots
beyond the bite
of ravenous rabbits

and when
the earth has
seen enough
and turns her face
toward darkness
—surrender

sleep and let
the bioware repair
and drifting
dream dreams
of other worlds
of van Leeuwenhoek's
society of the infinitesimal

see chaotic order there
the spinning darting way
of bacteria protists

nematodes and rotifers
seeking survival in
the kingdom of the invisible

now turn over
pull the blanket up
tuck it chin tight
and lift off
cruise the Milky Way
push on to galaxies
beyond

witness a star
in its death throes
fuel exhausted
core collapsing
outer layers expanding
thinning thinning
stretched and trembling
struggling
to contain the disorder
mounting in its core

and then
witness the explosion
like a colossal
over-blown balloon
behold
a red giant blossoms

a supernova of
frustration and anger
at the passing of the light
now circle and glide
like a swiveling
lion of the sea
through a billowing cloud
of red giant after-life
glowing in darkness

like a vast unblinking
blue-green eye
watching us
across the silence
of light years past
from a place
of new beginnings in
the birth place of the stars

Thinking of My Brother Jack

fall has fallen
winter is upon us

driving up a wet
winding road
to buy Christmas gifts
in the small gift shop
where the sweet

Trappist Nuns
of Mount Saint Mary's Abbey
sell the chocolate crunch
they create
in the fullness of silence

along the road
the trees
rooted solitary creatures
wear a white dressing
of snow
like the white habits
of the abbey's silent sisters

it seems
only a moment ago
that sap flowed freely
branches bursting
in green vitality
now stand
bare wiry and thin

and Jack in his last days
joined the trees
to whisper
an ageless wisdom
to me

for everything
a season . . .
a time to live

and a time to die

The Warmth of Her Waist

the air is pulsing
vibrations
now soft and gentle
as fingers
touching fanning
the shivering strings
of a harp

or the edgy energy
of salsa sounds
birthing
shimmies shakes
and swaying hips
evoking a tide of
pressing emotion
driving the need
to move
to become music

the delight
in discovering
another who
hears and feels
the siren song
the call to dance

the urge to share
infusing each . . .
the dance begins
with the dancer
within

shall we dance

in a shared movement
two creatures
seemingly attached
like schools of shiners
or murmurating starlings
expanding contracting
swooping and rising
in the moment
of union

coming together
hands extended
touching
his arm curled
in the warmth
of her waist
her hand
on his shoulder

two spirits
intermingled
two bodies
embracing
in a mutuality
of movement
a rising silver moon
sharing the warmth
of a golden setting sun

waves of sound
cresting falling
an inflowing tide

of melody and emotion
riffing in movement
bodies parting twirling
parting twirling
coming together
again and again
and again

finding freedom
expression and
release in the
sweet pain
of shared intimacy
an unspoken dialogue
in a near bodyless
otherworldly glide

. . . somewhere
Terpsichore
is humming
smiling swaying
side to side

The Rain of Sunshine

It's spring
cruising the inside lane
on route 495
what I think of as Me
is drifting in a cozy state
of day dream
while another part
a sort of
big brother within
attends the wheel

along the highway
a stand of trees
is waking from
a month's long sleep

can you hear them
breathing
inhaling exhaling
juices flowing

can you hear
buds of muted rose
filling swelling
at the tip of every
naked limb

while
spidery roots spread

in the understory
sponging up
the rain of sunshine
color oozing everywhere

in the small garden
in front of my house
a silent crack
a bit of dark soil
tilting up

put your ear to
the ground
listen closely
can you hear
the folded shaft
of green pushing

a sprout
of daffodil
striving to straighten
to spring
into the light
to raise
a flaring flower
to sound
its yellow trumpet

The Night the Music Changed

I was fifteen
it was 1955
Tommy Wayne
Stevie and I
sat waiting curious
anxious to see
Blackboard Jungle

it was summer
a weekday night
there'd be pizza later
the lights dimmed
the curtain slid open
12-bar blues burst
in our ears

rock and roll
a pounding rhythm
such sound
Captain Bill
was counting up

one two
three o'clock
four o'clock
rock

standby Houston
taking off
with Bill Haley
and the Comets
in a blast of beat
I'm gonna
Rock Around the Clock

mainlining *rock*
I couldn't sit still
displaced in time
taken up hangin' on
I'd slipped the bonds
of ballroom dancing
waltzes foxtrots swing

Gershwin's *Summertime*
Louie's gravelly
C'est Si Bon
still so good . . . but
rock and roll ruled now
waving and bubbling
in my blood stream

in the gym
of my all-male
Catholic high school

—usually a forum
for athletic struggles
debate competitions
or assemblies
of hushed gatherings
of pride or humiliation
where students stood
to hear their grades

read aloud
a mirror of days to come
in Marine Corps bootcamp

but on Friday nights
the space
was transformed
into a temple
of rock and roll

Gerry Lee Lewis
Elvis and others
rocked the cinder blocks
in the gym foundation
surely you could
feel it pulse

sweat soaked dancers
whirled twirled

and during ballads
became one
hot bellies touching

a Jesuit priest
hands behind his back
cruised
like an ice skater
gliding among the dancers
whispering
leave room for the Holy Ghost

—they didn't

The Outing

it's cloudy
wind whistling across
the small town common
mid-October
the air brisk
trees wearing coats
of fading green
pale yellow
striking golds
popping orange
and purple
softening into rose

a man sits chilled
on a metal bench
waiting for a woman
it's many years since
their summer-times
of dark-green and
leafy fullness
now their seasons
are coming to a close

the sun
is breaking through
the man inhales deeply
his lungs
and nose filling
with the earthy fragrance
of autumn's ripeness
and decay

he muses
can the barren trees
of winter be far away

he feels a presence
nearby
a woman's voice asks
is this seat taken
turning he says
no please join me

sixty years earlier
the woman sent
the man a letter
she would marry another

in the mating dance
of those early years
the man a boy really
was like a moth
dancing in the warmth
of a lantern glowing in
summer darkness
and wishing
to continue the dance

the woman

perhaps sensing
the music may stop
would not be left standing

or maybe
she had found
a serious man
a man who had set
his dancing shoes aside

months before
while rummaging
through a jumble
of files and papers
the old man came across
several photos

photos of the woman
taken many years ago
in the days
of shared attraction

thinking she may
wish to have these
memories made manifest
he sent them to her

weeks passed
with no response
when one day
a letter appeared
in his mailbox
thanking him for the photos

pleased
the man responded

he wrote
would you like to
have a visit
a coffee
perhaps a chance to
swap stories
of paths not taken

and now they sit
by the common's edge
a quiet moment
two old friends
in autumn
on a cold hard bench

soon chatter and laughter
warms them and
fills the space of time
between their then
and their now

. . . all in the shadow
of the coming winter

Soul Singing

reading poems today
poems I've written
I find some
lovely touching
though strangely
unfamiliar
where did these words
come from . . .

*days of withering
individuality*

*in popcorn
flavored darkness*

merchants of rascality

*pulsating Parisian
pulchritude*

they came unbidden
have little to
do with me
more like the sound
of a soul singing

. . . humming

Saturday Morning Music

Saturday morning music. I am this music just now. Clair De Lune. Moonlight, a sound story of reflected light in darkness. In this moment hands hover, fingers search, touch the keyboard. Typing.

Another moment, but not. It's one. It's Now. Continuous. The feeling of feet on floor, arms sensing arm rests, bottom on the cushion, breathing. Being breathed. Susan's awake she says, *it's late, I set the alarm. Or maybe I didn't. I need to get the plants in the ground before it's too hot.*

Breakfast, routine, nothing is routine, all just happening. Set the table. Filter, coffee, add water, brew. Pan, bacon, cook. Eggs, crack, drain, set aside. Pan, fill, water, heat. Eggs to water with care. Poach. Fruit, slice, apples, pears, oranges, bananas and grapes.

Food into bowls, bowls onto plates. Steaming hot coffee, pour. Serve. Eat. Susan, in from garden, says, *that soil's too hard, need to deepen the hole, add some good stuff, make a welcome home for that plant. Feed it.*

I say, *I'll wash these dishes, and the Moon will reflect the Sun.*

Riding the Chaparral with Thunder

Christmas Eve day
a few flakes falling
landing lightly
on spikes of frozen grass
in the field behind
Dorchester High for Boys
Dot Chesta
in Boston speak

an eight-year-old boy
skipping
one hand beating
his hip
in galloping time
giddy up Thunder
giddy up Thunder
com'on boy
com'on boy

he's a Saturday afternoon
wrangler on the trail
dodging tumbling tumbleweed
a bandana snugged
over his nose
against dust and debris
he's crossing the chaparral

outside
the Codman Square theatre

he ties Thunder to the
hitching post
saunters
up to the box office
slides a quarter
thru the hole in the window
one ticket please . . . and
a shot of sarsaparilla

settling
in his balcony seat
he tucks his legs
under him
wrapped in popcorn
flavored darkness
above the dreamers
in their high rent seats
below

invisible hands
part the curtains
their trailing ends
swinging
like the skirt
of a whirling dervish

high above
the cinema dreamers
deep in his hidey-hole

the projectionist
flips a switch

spinning reels
clatter to life and
the wild world
of dry-gulchers
bushwhackers
chaps spurs
palominos pintos
and paints
sliding sidewinders
swinging tavern doors
and sailing
prairie schooners
come to life on
the screen

two hours later
a stagecoach
races and rattles
toward a cliff
at the edge
of a plateau

to be continued

appears and
credits begin to roll

the buckaroo
mounts up
making his way home

in his living room
the scent
of Christmas tree drifts

diluting kerosene fumes
from the cast iron
stove in the kitchen

the tree seems alive
a strange visitor
from another dimension
sparkling in blues
greens whites and reds
branches bent
with dangling strips
of tinsel and wearing
a star on his head

the boy stands
looking out the
window of the
second-floor apartment
wind whistling
a wintery tune
snowy sleet
slashing sideways

in the spattered
darkness below
a lamplighter
lifts a pole shaped
like a shepherd's crook
and fires the gas
in a street lamp

a halo of flickering light
bursts in the cold
December night

in a pile of packages
beneath the tree
the boy reads one
labelled Joey
it's heavy
something moves
in the box
when he shakes it

at first light
on Christmas day
he can see
prints in the snow
left by the lamplighter
dousing his gaslight
in the early morning gray

finding the package
marked Joey
he tears the wrapping
there it is
a six-shooter cap gun
belt and holster
much like the one
he'd seen in W.T. Grant's
with his Mum
in Codman Square
a few weeks ago

Regarding Marriage

I pray
that God blesses
you with gentle
honest insight

insight that
leads you
to understand
the nature of love

insight that leads
you to see more clearly
the person you call
yourself

insight that reveals
the walls we erect
to defend our ego
that false sense of self

insight to see
that beyond the
barriers of ego
flows a reflection of
God we call Self

insight to sense
the shared exposure
of our physical
and spiritual
vulnerabilities

insight to see
that today two
have become One
in a newborn Unity

insight to see
this infant Unity
is fragile requires
care and nurture

insight to see that
care and nurture
flow freely from
the fountainhead
of Self

insight to see
that when two
become One
we too take part
in God's Love
and Creation

January Nights in Northern Virginia

Susan paused
in folding the
still warm laundry

she held up two socks
an odd pair
both green
but one fuzzy
the other smooth
one short
the other long

I love those socks
they bring me back
to my military days
when they warmed
tender young toes
on frosty January nights
in northern Virginia

how did they come
to be separated
domestic detectives
the world over
have pondered this
question but the mystery
still mystifies
heads are scratched
eyes lose focus

neurons fire
speculation bounces
off cranial walls

no doubt
they started out
wrapped in each other
like lovers
a happy pair of socks
content with keeping
the toes and ankles
of a lucky biped
warm and toasty
peas in a pod
you may say
they were living
the fullness
of life as a sock

while deep
in their threadful
hearts they honored
the universal anthem
of sockdom
sock it to 'em
sock it to 'em
sock it to 'em

perhaps the
pair was rent asunder
by dark forces
swirling in
their home drawer
perhaps knee high
and thigh high stockings
sophisticated coverings

with anti-military
aspirations conspired to
disappear the mates

or could it be
the once-matched pair
became separated
in the chugging waters
of the washer
lost and failing
to reunite in the dryer
. . . the horror

did frowning luddites
linger near
decrying the loss
of matched pairs as
yet another curse
given us by
the industrial revolution

now separated
and back
in their drawer
did they pine for
their lost partners
descending into
into socky despair

or unmatched
though they were
could they rally
becoming a sort of
unity in function

a funky sort of
e pluribus unum
could the two
become one in
a comforting compromise
so rare in these days

of withering individuality

Here They Come

No arms
bodies like oversized
feathered footballs
perched on scaley
celery-stalk legs

Deliberate in their
toe walking way
exuding a regal air
of vague disdain
lifting placing
lifting placing

Small
featherless heads
piston as they stride
red engorged flesh
dangling from
snooded beaks

Serpentine necks
extend like periscopes
twisting and turning
on their axes

In rafters they come
turkey talking
strutting their stuff
in a down fifth avenue
Easter sort of way

Color changing dewlaps
like mood rings
swing beneath their chins
the bigger and brighter
the better
flashing signals that
toms are on the march
and looking for love

Their chests puffing
and looking like
tweedledum and tweedledee
moving slowly
turning this way and that

Snapping tail fans
of upright iridescent
rainbow-colored feathers
like a card dealer
fanning his deck

At the slightest sign
of interest they scoot
in the direction
of mostly indifferent
yet curious hens

It's an old game
in the world
but for some
it's always the same
. . . flash and size matter

You Can't Take It with You
. . . Really

he wandered the world
from the deserts of Baja
to hill station Mussoorie
in the mountains
of Dehra Doon
art was his passport

and now began
his most
arduous adventure

he prepared by
giving things away
his paintings
a twenty-year-old
Ford Ranger pickup
money

thick fillets
of freshly caught
striped bass
half-liter jugs of
caramel flavored cider

my brother Jack
a man of faith
indulged his appetites

yet never clung to
or valued
the stuff of the world

he was
as the old
teaching taught
in the world
but not of the world

what he couldn't
give away
was taken from him
with relentless insistence

weight was taken
voice was taken
taste was taken
sleep was taken

and finally
that mysterious force
that supports a life
worth living
his energy was taken

and yet
even as the light
he cast grew dim

he offered coffee
and cooked
a meal for me
never defiant
never knowing
if he'd have

the courage
to live each day
inch by inch
and see his course
through to the end

in our quiet
conversations
he often said

we'll see

or
*what is needed
will be given*

or
*if it's for you
it won't go by you*

one day
another breath

was needed

if it's for you
it won't go by you

Flaming Mother in the Darkness

standing
by the kitchen window
a brush stroke of pink
paints the western sky

scattered splashes
of darkish clouds
edges aflame
drift in the radiance
of the sinking Sun

the Sun aglow
in crushing fusion
its energy
pulsing pulsing
as if alive

our star
a flaming mother
in the darkness
gifting her life
and light to earth
is herself
a miracle of balance

compressed by
the god of gravity
into a small
tight ball

while in her core
nuclear fuel blazes
pushes back

I wonder what's for supper . . .

For Susan My Valentine

Today a day
Set aside
To speak of love

What sort of love
I wonder
Sexual filial fraternal

Yes love has many faces
It's a thousand-petalled
Lotus unfolding

Like the lotus
You slowly
Revealed yourself

See a doe in the
Underbrush shy
Lifting her head

To look
At he who looks
How can he but

Love

Images Flicker and Fade

Sunday afternoon
sun shining
Miles Davis
making love to his horn

I am deep
in the magic of mind
conjuring words
painting images that
flicker and fade
in a tangle of neurons

it's been like Alaska
here 'bouts
people wrapped
in thick coats and
wearing stocking hats
striding with deliberation
trailing steamy contrails

women gather
talk of children
make muffins
drink tea
conversations
sweeten life

elsewhere
men and women shiver

hunker down
in scraped out
frozen holes

blowing meager
warmth on fingers
white and numb
while overhead
shells spin
whistle and rifle
through cloudless
skies of blue

striking and shaking
the aching earth
death is dropping
on men on women
on children

buildings totter
walls and windows gone
lives exposed
like dangling entrails

Piecing the Universe Together

behold a box
of jigsawed puzzle pieces
open to reveal

a microcosm of chaos
seeking order
a universe in miniature

a jumble
of unrelated pieces
or so it seems

impose order
onto chaos
arrange a frame

of border pieces
reduce infinity
to manageable bits

within the frame
examine each piece
relative to the whole

trying failing
and trying yet again
until one piece

is joined to another

and bit by bit
an image is forming

revealing dogs
cats butterflies
barns books
and barrels
tractors hay stacks
boats and bicycles
flowers and trees
black holes
constellations
and galaxies

infinity is puzzling

Hiroshima Bodhisattva

at the bus stop
outside their hotel
an old man
his daughter and
two granddaughters
boarded a crowded bus
to the Shinkansen Line
in Kyoto Station

as they tapped
their Suica cards
on the fare reader
a small woman sat
watching in silence

the daughter took
a seat next to the
woman who watched

older than our travelers
the woman was
perhaps a baby when
the bomb exploded
over Hiroshima
creating a moment
of Hell on Earth

the brim of her
red pork pie hat

turned up
a cable of grey
braided hair

creased the collar
of her white blouse
and fell to the edge
of a hip-length
brown vest
baggy blue trousers
gathered at the ankles
above black and white
hi-top PF Fliers

crinkled eyes twinkling
the old woman
leaned her smile close
to the daughter's ear
and in the spirit
of a bodhisattva
whispered
you don't pay until
you leave the bus
the daughter nodded

leaving the bus
the travelers mounted
moving stairs
to rise above Kyoto's
quiet bustle

as they rose
every silent soul
kept left

those who hurried
passed with ease
on the right

cresting
the stairs melted
into the station platform
pouring its riders into
a skybourne
aquifer of humanity

living rivers
of souls schooled
in each direction
subtle moves
made for mixing
without collision
there was no
sorry excuse me
or *watch it*

the space of alien
sounds and symbols
spoke sparingly
in our traveler's

language with
offerings of *this way*
information and *exit*

paralyzed
before a turnstile
the travelers rudderless
and uncertain

which of two tickets
they should use
clock ticking
their train approaching

when the bodhisattva
materialized in
pork pie hat
upturned brim
and PF Fliers

questions asked
and quickly answered
this ticket not that
proper tickets
fed to the turnstile

swallowed and digested
halting paddles
burped open

the foursome
quickstepped
boarding a train
which had an engine
shaped like a
platypus head
and a body like
an atlas rocket

the doors
slid silently shut

and the bullet train
shot off
to Hiroshima

hours later
they wandered about
ground zero in
Hiroshima Memorial
Peace Park
where 78 years ago
the secret energy
of the atoms
was unleashed
in a flash
brighter and hotter

than the sun
incinerating 70,000
humans in an instant
and slowly killing
60,000 more in time

where were you then
bodhisattva bodhisattva

Time Traveler

sitting alone
on the edge of his bed
an old man
flips through his
high school yearbook
class of 1957
a time capsule

he considers
. . . attend or not attend
a reunion luncheon
of seven or eight classmates

where are all the others

flip flip flip
pages passing
he pauses
his picture
a note

*Joe loves
our record hops
travels many miles
to reach our school
on the boulevard
hopes to study
social work in the fall*

Joe
born to a family

of blue-collar Irish
money scarce
as hen's teeth
stood
at the end of a line
of six older sisters
he'd have what
was never offered
to them

a chance to climb

his white-haired mum
would earn his tuition
caring for old people
in their homes

he was handed over
to the Jesuits
taking his place
in an all-male
Catholic high school
in Boston.

he sits staring
adrift in thought

in the stillness
he becomes

a time traveler
in the dream-like
land of times past

paying his way with
small withdrawals
from the bank
of memories

an image is forming
the entire student body
is gathered
in the gymnasium
of Boston College
High School

Fr. 'Mouse' Mahoney
clad in a black cassock
from neck to toe
and barely reaching
the microphone
is standing on a podium
scanning the assembly
of anxious faces

he calls for silence
in a voice
bigger than he
the coughing

foot shuffling
and chair scraping
stops

he reads a name

a student slowly stands
the first of many
and in the standing
seems to shrink

*as his grades
are read aloud* . . .

another memory
muscles forward
it's a cold Friday night
light snow is falling
there's a *record hop*
in that same gymnasium

girls
from the girl's
schools around Boston
chattering laughing
flowed into the hall
taking up position
across the dance floor
facing the wall of boys

inside it's toasty
soon the heat
will be rising
in the wake
of dancing
rocking couples

the disc jockey
spins a seven-inch
45 rpm single
vinyl disc

Little Richard
is raisin' the rafters
electrifying the air with
"Good Golly Miss Molly"

the old man
sees himself dancing
again and again
with a smallish
smiling girl

during
the slow dancing
he holds her close
he's in love

he searches for her
at the next dance

and the next
and the next
never forgetting

or ever seeing her again

Unseen Fingers

it's his birthday
the grandfather reflects
85 birthdays . . . hmmmm

a gentle winter's day
sitting on the deck outside
bundled and warm

he's distracted
by a commotion
images light and dark
flashing on the floor
near his chair

a small circle
of black busy shadows
shaped like the citizens
in a drop of pond water

hydra paramecium
divers darters
wiggling waggling
merrily waving
their long thin flagella

his gaze tracks up
to a mobile
hanging nearby
small plastic

circles and squares
dangle and twist
stirred by unseen fingers
of sun-warmed winter air

and birthing
black shadowy
phantoms morphing
like bubbles bursting
on the floor
near his chair

bat like images
seeming to skitter
through the scene
like floaters in the
corner of your eye

drifting

he wonders
about his deathday

The Coils of Cochlea

Vivaldi's Winter
is playing
whirling welling
harmonies

a typhoon of notes
a dancing melody
bursting from
cresting waves of sound
as in a tidal rush
racing into
the Bay of Fundy

flowing into my ears
round and round
in the snail-shaped
coils of cochlea

passing on over
micro-plains
of waving stereocilia
like wind wafting
on a world of wheat

I'm afloat
on sea of sound
drifting in the infinite
silence of Self

is it the magic
of biology or

is the *Musician*
playing me
like a harp
with fingers of grace

On Memorial Day a Bluebird's Song
Drifts in the Silence

Sitting outside
in stillness a dawning
a swelling sense
of the fullness of life
. . . awe filled

piercing the silence
a Bluebird's
crystalline song
drifts
in a stand of trees
rooted in solitude
just beyond my deck

from the house
a sound
Eva Cassidy
singing softly
in tones of
bitter sweet sadness
she hears
songs of love
. . . but not for her

oh me oh my
everything changing
nothing remains the same
nothing to cling to

just a flow
and a letting go

She Whispers to Me

Sonos hums
in the background
Joe Bongiorno
true to his name
brings good
to the morning

his fingers
high stepping
over the ivories
of a toothy keyboard
unlocking the
sweet-sad sound
of *Resilience*

the sun is sitting
at its apogee
content
and casting radiance
on the venetian blind
across my room
painting vinyl slats
with sunshine
till the topmost slat
gleams with delight

the shine is intense
I close my eyes
and there
in the darkness

a column
of emerald green
shimmers
in the afterglow

now the intensity of
the shine is sliding
across the slats
as the planet
does her dervish dance

turning her face
from the source of life
she whispers
her wisdom to me

don't fret
nothing lasts forever
boyo

Dream Driving

it's autumn again
dream driving
south along the highway

the sky is deep blue
the long road ahead
narrows, rises slightly
piercing a paler blue
at the horizon

yoking back the wheel
tires spin off the tarmac
the car noses up

at altitude
clouds are scattered
carefree casual
bright edgy tops
are ragged
like fly away hair

gliding now
the breathing
multi-colored
quilt of rooted
creatures that
covers and warms
the shoulder
of the highway

is quietly beginning
to shed its dying
leaves of orange reds
and browns and
coming in time
to stand like naked
gray skeletons

banking hard left
drifting over
my backyard
the air teems with life

feeders filled
to spilling welcome
migrating birds
white-throated
sparrows
yellow-rumped
warblers and
red-winged
blackbirds

beat their wings
batter the air
in flitting
avian madness
with deep dives
popping ascents

and careening
crisscrosses
from here
visibility is maximum

humanity is bleeding
everywhere

Sadness in the Trees

springtime it's raining
a moment
of new beginnings
but there's sadness
in the trees
wet leaves heavy
drooping

they've seen so much
these silent witnesses
poisoning
of their planetary gardens
desecration of
earth's rolling oceans
obscene assaults
on ancient forests

yet still they stand
muted masses in
a multitude of shapes
and colors
gentle greens
soft banana yellows
orange-reds
pinks like juicy
Georgia peaches
light browns
bleeding into beiges
oaks both
black and white

they live
pressed together
yet apart
each struggling
to share the same
life-giving light
and fertile earth

while the world
of man seems
to be coming apart

A Perfect Woman to Be Dating

there's a place
on every computer
where even
the most socially
isolated can find
at least digital
reassurance that
they have not
been forgotten

. . . and never will be

in an otherwise
indifferent world
self-appointed
agents of happiness
are lurking
in the junk mail

firing off indiscriminate
reminders and
florid expressions
of concern
digital missives
crafted to manipulate
perceived weakness

these offerings
dispatched

in the hope of
filling a cornucopia
of unrecognized needs

*try our chocolate pancakes
and never gain a pound
—act today*

*I like romantic men
shall I post you
a few candid photos*

*I am the perfect woman
to be dating
I wear spurs . . . dude
and I'm ready
to be the one you desire*

*tired of being called
a turkey-necked
old geezer*

*need new luxurious sheets
liver detox
Nasa eclipse glasses
a pinched nerve fix
hearing aids*

call us today

*you'll soon be swanning
with the rest of the flock*

you may say
*but junk mail
is only the curse of our day*
perhaps not

idle iconoclasts
spin a tale
that long long ago
Nathaniel Emmons
prominent New England
theologian of the day
gathered a group
of grey hairs
from the Second Church
to choose a name
for their newly
incorporated town

it was decided
to name their little village
the town of Franklin
after Benjamin Franklin
printer patriot philosopher
. . . a*nd much more*

the grey hairs

recognizing the
potential moral value
of offering this honor
fired off a request
to olde Ben

how's about buying us
a set of belfry bells
for the steeple
of our meetinghouse

Ben being
an American intellectual
. . . and nobody's fool
may have felt that
the church people
were well aware of
. . . and intent on mining
the olde patriot's
rumored pursuit
of pulsating Parisian
pulchritude

they were offering
a portal for repentance
while hoping
to bring home the bacon
in the form of
bells for their belfry

clever lad that he was
Ben wondered whether
the grey hairs might have
bats in their belfry

but after a bit
of reflection
he suspected he may
be the target
of colonial junk mail

but rather than deleting
the request

he did a switcheroo
sending instead
a set of books
and a note saying

sense
is preferable to sound

the books remain
on display this very day
in the Franklin Public Library
. . . that Ben oh my

His Arms Open Wide

agitation in the trees
fingers of wind
lift leaves
their undersides
reflecting the silver-gray
of turbulent skies

in such moments
my thoughts drift
where is my brother
Jack
he was here
now he's gone

so strange
we talked and walked
many hours in memory
he was dying
I was the older brother
by ten years

he said to me once
you don't know
how important
you were as my
big brother

I didn't know

he hoped that he
would have the
courage to live
with clear attention
to be present
unclouded by
medications or denial
living until he died

when he could no
longer swallow easily
he gave me
his bread
his lettuce
his apples
his pears

from time to time
he was visited by
the death demon
 what if

*what if the pain
becomes too much
to bear*

*what if I try
to take a breath
and can't . . .*

the last time
we were together
his breathing heavy
the sound of
a bastard rasp
drawn across a
metal edge
violating the silence
of the room

he sat in his rocking chair
legs akimbo
quadriceps ravaged
knees knobs boney prominent

I stood to leave
he struggled to stand
we always hugged
when I left

he slumped back in the chair
threw his arms open
hugged me as best he could
goodbye Joey he said

the goodbye
the arms open wide

About the Author

Joe Leary was born in Boston, grew up in Franklin, Massachusetts, and still lives there. He has written for pleasure all his life. He has published articles and book chapters in the field of dental implantology. He started writing poetry in 2017. His first book of poetry was *'til the well runs dry* (Kelsay Books, 2024).

His non-literary experience includes service as a Marine, an FBI agent, Periodontist, teacher, and parent; and other important experience as a grocery clerk, floor washer, mill worker, hospital attendant, pathology lab worker, and more. With such varied life experience, you can imagine he comes with a rich source of material for his work.

Themes of this work are wide-ranging: humor, family relationships, self-knowledge, and the beauty of nature.

www.ingramcontent.com/pod-product-compliance
Lightning Source LLC
Chambersburg PA
CBHW071010160426
43193CB00012B/1997